# Look Before

# You Leap

## A Guide for Aspiring Lawyers

By Chris Hargreaves

Copyright 2013

# Table of Contents

# INTRODUCTION

I am a person who likes to know about things before I get too far into them. That goes for buying a DVD player, going to a movie, and it was true for my legal career also.

One resource that I would have greatly appreciated while I attempted to pick my University preferences and discern my preferred career was a resource with some practical knowledge about what it was like to work in a law firm, what a legal career looked like in reality, and which answered some of the frequently distributed misinformation about what it was actually like to take up a career in the law.

I have been fortunate throughout my career to have had mentors and guiding senior practitioners who have been prepared to share that practical knowledge and insight with me, but I know that not all junior practitioners or aspiring law students are so lucky. For that reason, I have written this short book with a view to providing some hands-on explanation of what a real career in a law firm looks like, what you can expect in some areas, what a "normal" career path looks like in terms of private practice, and addressing some of the common hopes or concerns that young people might have about going into the law.

I have not assumed that you know or do not know anything. Where necessary I have attempted to explain any jargon that I use, or terms that might be commonplace in the legal industry but not necessarily anywhere else (a glass of *mutatis mutandis*, anyone, or would you prefer a nice *nunc pro tunc*?)

Whether you are a high school student, a university student, an early career law clerk or young lawyer, I hope that this book might address some of those issues which you may have been wanting addressed, but not necessarily known who you can go to for answers.

None of the information in this book is an "industry secret" or any such nonsense, but a lot of it is information that you might not otherwise be able to get in one sitting, or information that traditionally has found its way from person to person through means other than by way of a short guide like this one.

The contents of this book are obviously based on my personal experience. In many instances the experiences of others will be different, although I have endeavoured to present information that is widely accepted and representative of current practice. You may find that the details will vary from place to place, or that others provide you with different information or even direct contradiction to my own thoughts in this book. I don't consider that a bad thing – gather all the information you can, including those from disagreeing sources, and identify for yourself how you want to use that information to best advantage in your decision making.

I have found my legal career to be rewarding on many levels. Although some of the information presented here can be daunting, I hope that at least it is honest and representative of what a real lawyer does with their time, their career, their attitude and their colleagues.

I welcome questions, comments, criticisms or observations about this book, or suggestions for future books (or revisions of this one). My contact details can be found at the end.

# WHY BE A LAWYER?

---

*"Up until 35 I had a slightly skewed world view. I honestly believed everybody in the world wanted to make abstract paintings, and people only became lawyers and doctors and brokers and things because they couldn't make abstract paintings." - Frank Stella*

---

Hopefully as you have progressed in your life so far, you have gotten into the habit of reasoning (at least a little) with yourself about the question: why?

Asking yourself why you want to do something, and taking the time to articulate a proper and honest answer, can be a stark wake up call to some who have headed for so long in a particular direction that they actually don't understand the reasons for it anymore (or never had any reasons in the first place). I strongly recommend you do it: now. In fact, after you read this chapter, stop reading for a bit and go and have a proper think about why it is that you actually want to be a lawyer. Take notes if that helps.

A decision to take up legal studies and then a subsequent decision to begin a career in the law is potentially long term, and not to be taken lightly. You are doing yourself a distinct disservice if you don't carefully consider your motivation for doing it, and then examine whether that motivation is really going to give you the incentive you need.

The sections below set out some particular areas which commonly come up as motivating factors for pursuing a career in the law, as well as my thoughts on the accuracy or otherwise of them.

## Money

What television has taught us is that all lawyers (irrespective of their youth) are on enourmous salaries, can afford lovely places to live, expensive wine and cocktails, and a constant array of gorgeous clothes (or, if not, are going to get a very lucrative job offer next episode). I've also noticed that television law firms hire only attractive people.

For those who haven't realised it yet (or have optimistically chosen to ignore the obvious), the television portrayal of a legal career is grossly misleading.

It must be said, however, that over the long term a legal career can be financially rewarding. Let's put that general comment into some real life perspective.

According to the Australian Bureau of Statistics, the average weekly full time earnings, as at November 2012, for persons in Australia was $1,458.00 per week (this figure is pre-tax, but excludes superannuation). This equates to roughly an average full time salary in Australia of $76,024.28, excluding superannuation.

That figure, however, is a bit out of whack because it also includes the "uber wealthy" category of individuals, who have a tendency in Australia to drag the average figures up.

Therefore, a more pragmatic figure to look at (in my view) is the median earning figure. For the 2010/2011 financial year (the most recent available at the time of writing) the Australian median individual earning figure was $48,684. You can get more information should you want it at http://www.ato.gov.au/taxstats.

Now let's compare that to a legal career. Everything I am about to say is based on industry averages and massive generalisations. It is not gospel and it should create neither false hope nor false concerns in anybody. Ultimately, in a law firm, you will be paid what it is worth to the firm to keep you. If that figure doesn't match up closely enough with what you think you are worth, then a discussion can be had or you can leave. If it does match up, then you should be happy.

The most reasonably sized salary survey available at the time of writing is the Hays Salary Survey 2013, upon which the figures I am about to cite are based. All of the figures include superannuation, bonuses, professional memberships and the like. There are a number of free salary surveys similar to the Hays one released each year, primarily by recruitment agencies. As such they should be treated cautiously.

I would also point out that by the time you are a "graduate" you have done 4-5 years at uni and maybe have some work experience as well. In that 4-5 years while you earned nothing, your friends who have done diesel fitting apprenticeships have been earning pretty decent cash and your own bank balance has been left for dead. For that reason, comparing the "starting" salary of a graduate to the first year apprentice salary is like comparing apples with... chicken kiev. You are also about to start repaying government loans (unless you were lucky enough to pay upfront for university, or have a benevolent parent pay it for you) to the tune of around $40,000 to $50,000.

A graduate in a small private practice in Brisbane can hope to earn somewhere between $40,000 and $55,000 including superannuation. That figure will creep gradually upwards in your first few years, and over time you might hope to achieve a salary of around $115,000 by your sixth year after admission, and something over $180,000 should you manage to reach partner level.

In real terms, you should expect that the seminars, professional memberships and other costs included in those indicative figures will take away at least $2,000 per year, as well as factoring in the 9% (9.25% from July 2013, going upwards towards 12%) superannuation component that is built in to get to what you actually take home.

In contrast, in a large national (often called "top tier") law firm, your graduate salary might be closer to the $55k to $69k range, and by the time you hit your sixth year post admission you might hope for around $140,000, followed with a pretty attractive salaried partner earnings of what is described as "$250k+".

You might immediately think in response that you will be aiming for a job in a "top tier" firm. That's all well and good, but there are a few hurdles along the way. First – competition for graduate positions in such firms is fierce. You might want a job in a "top tier" firm, but that doesn't mean they want you. Second – graduate staff turnover (the rate at which people are fired or leave) is traditionally quite high in such firms. Third - unsurprisingly, attractive salary comes with certain expectations; you will work hard, you will likely work long hours (although not always) and the expectations placed upon you in exchange for the handsome salary you are earning will likely be higher. Fourth – opportunities to excel and "stand out from the crowd" in firms become less as the size of the firm increases. The greater the size of your peer group the more difficult it is for you to differentiate yourself.

Smaller and medium sized firms should not be discounted only on the issue of money (in my view). Choosing where to work should take a holistic approach, with money only being one aspect. Examine any potential firm on its own merits, its people, its policies and its quality. Each firm, irrespective of size, has its strong and its weak points.

There you have it.

In my view, law is not different from any other professional career when it comes to money. You often start at a fairly plain level, but if you are prepared to put in the work then the opportunities at the other end are quite attractive.

# Power and Influence

Another lesson from television is that as a lawyer you will gain the magical ability to make people do what you want them to do. This will notionally be achieved through your superior intellect (all television lawyers are, apparently, academic overachievers), the massive resources at your disposal, your sheer rat cunning, your awesome knowledge of the law and your ability to be extremely persuasive and cajole somebody into ultimately either agreeing with you or doing what you want even if they don't agree.

Once again, this might be a slight glamourisation of what the legal profession is like. That said, as a lawyer and trusted advisor you will find that clients will look to you over time for advice, guidance and recommendations; and will often do what you suggest.

Power is the authority to direct and manage resources, including human resources, with a view to achieving a particular result.

Influence is the ability to change at a more fundamental level the way a person thinks or acts.

The two go hand in hand, although neither is a requirement of the other. I could be powerful, in that I might be a managing partner of a firm and people will do what I say, but I might also be simultaneously unable to convince anybody to change in any way – they only do what I ask because of my authority.

Similarly a junior staff member may have significant influence by virtue of their ability to create a strong argument for a particular course of action, but ultimately may lack the power to implement such a course of action without the imprimatur of their superiors.

Power and influence are compelling motivators because they give the holder of those qualities a significant boost in their sense of self-worth, and the feeling of exercising power or influence successfully can contribute to a satisfying sense of accomplishment. We see an example of this in bullying (a misuse of power). The bully seeks to use their power to make themselves feel good, but rather than use their power in a way that is constructive, they do it in the way that is destructive.

An important factor for students, graduates and junior lawyers to understand is that although they may lack institutional power for a time, they do not lack influence.

Power, in particular within a traditional law firm hierarchy, generally comes down the track. However the ability of young lawyers and graduates to influence their workplace is significant, and not just in ways limited to the actual practice of law going on around them.

Lawyers at all levels can influence the morale of a group significantly. A positive attitude towards work and colleagues will have significant influence on your work environment. Obviously the opposite is also true, with negativity being pervasive and ultimately destructive within a workplace.

Similarly, young lawyers can easily impact the culture of a workgroup in terms of work quality. If a young lawyer consistently produces extremely high quality work, then that will have a positive impact on the others in the team. It will provide a greater sense of purpose, of integrity, of pride and ultimately of satisfaction resulting from a job well done.

Positive attitude and high quality work will also, naturally, gain the gratitude and positive attention from your superiors who, in my experience, do not take long to sort out the "pecking order" of junior practitioners when it comes to these things.

So if you are of the view that these aspects of power and influence are significant motivators for you, then I would encourage you to look at the ways you can get satisfaction out of these areas even in your formative years as a young lawyer. You may lack the title or the standing to be the decision maker for a time, but you still contribute significantly to the workplace in many ways, and in that sense your influence with everyone you meet is tangible and meaningful.

Over time your positive contributions and influence will be paired with opportunities to exert power, and your investment in positively influencing outcomes in your early years will have been worthwhile as you combine that with your new found authority.

# Intellectual Stimulation

The practice of law can be an amazingly stimulating environment.

It can also be so tedious that you would feel more alive by slipping into a coma for the day.

So as to not create unrealistic expectations about the practice of law, I wanted to give some practical views on my experiences about what practice as a solicitor is like.

Personally I find law to be an extremely satisfying and stimulating area to work in. I find the questions that I am faced with on a day to day basis to be very interesting, and the occasional peaks of stress and urgency add enough flavour into my week without pushing me over the edge.

What day to day legal practice is NOT, however, is a constant flurry of urgent phone calls and trips to Court for injunctions with paper flying everywhere, judges running in any out of chambers yelling at people and clients with never ending amounts of money prepared to throw it all in your direction for the purposes of "winning".

The reality of legal practice is actually more benign, which I accept may be a disappointment to many readers. Below is an average set of standard tasks that a lawyer might have to complete with an indication of frequency. Although I have endeavoured to keep the list non-specific so far as practice area, it obviously comes from my personal experience in the litigation field, and so there are no doubt some items missing and others which may exist only for those in the same area. There is an * next to those illustrious tasks to which junior lawyers and law clerks are frequently delegated or have to participate in.

- Filling out file opening forms (weekly)
- Reviewing printouts of potential conflict checks on file opening (weekly);
- Providing estimates and client agreements to clients (weekly if not daily);
- Requesting clients deposit funds to the trust account (as often as needed);
- Reviewing invoices and chasing up payment (if you forgot the step above) (as often as needed);
- Asking the client for more (or any) information or documentation (weekly);
- Answering calls or emails from clients (daily);
- Drafting documents – Court proceedings, contracts, deeds, transfer documents (daily);
- *Preparing lists of documents for disclosure (litigation only) (fortnightly)
- Submitting documents to State Revenue for duty imprints or returns (frequency depends on your area);
- *Preparing briefs to counsel and indexing them (fortnightly);
- Meetings with clients or counsel (every day or couple of days);
- Going to Court (maybe once a fortnight, if you're in a litigious area, more if you do a lot of debt collection/insolvency/bankruptcy style work);

- Drafting advices or updates to clients (daily);
- Reviewing status of files and ensuring that they are in order (daily);
- *Completing time sheets (all the time);
- *Internal Meetings – group, marketing, firm-wide, committee (twice weekly);
- *Writing articles and papers (monthly if not more often);
- *Research (daily in some areas, less often in others).

Hopefully this list helps you out with the realities of legal practice in a law firm. As you can see, many of the tasks are not too exciting, although the interest level will often depend on the topic or specifics of the individual task.

Don't take away from the above that legal practice is mind numbingly dull – far from it. The sheer range of tasks in which to be engaged is fairly interesting of itself. But be prepared for reality, so that when you hit the ground in a law firm you are not completely shocked by the lack of adrenaline from time to time.

# Helping People

It seems corny to put this in, but a very real motivator for a lot of lawyers is to help people. Legal training and expertise provides a solid foundation for service to your community.

Regrettably, that ideal is often lost in the commercial reality of legal practice, where the underlying goal of helping people can be lost in the spicy gumbo that is legal practice. Issues such as legal costs and "butt covering" can quickly turn an idealistic young lawyer into a professional cynic.

That transition is a common outcome, but not a mandatory one.

If helping people is a motivator for you, then legal practice is an excellent way to achieve that goal.

However, you need to be aware that your ability to help people will be fettered by the way your firm practices. It may mean that you can't help everyone who might need it, or that you end up helping people who you don't particularly care for.

Having a genuine desire to help your clients is also a beneficial marketing trait. Clients and prospects respond to people who are genuinely interested in helping them solve their legal issues (disingenuous or feigned interest can have the opposite effect).

Over time, you will also have a greater ability to influence the specific kind of work you are doing and the clients that you are serving. If helping a particular category of people is high on your wish list, then you might have a chance to do that.

Your desire to help people need not be limited to your law firm, of course. You can volunteer for legal organizations that assist self-represented litigants. You can also get involved in community and charitable organizations, where your critical thinking, research and communication abilities will generally be highly valued. For the same reasons, many lawyers find themselves serving on boards or management committees, where legal skills (not just legal knowledge) can be useful.

Therefore, even if private legal practice does not tick off on this motivating factor for you, there are many extra-curricular opportunities which can be used to fill that desire.

# CHARACTERISTICS OF A GOOD LAWYER

---

*"Nobody wants to read about the honest lawyer down the street who does real estate loans and wills. If you want to sell books, you have to write about the interesting lawyers - the guys who steal all the money and take off. That's the fun stuff." - John Grisham*

---

This chapter sets out my opinion of some fundamental character qualities that make a good lawyer. Often these are not learned traits, although I see no particular reason why they cannot be so. More importantly these qualities are those which relate to the underlying character of the individual. Although law school can teach you a certain amount of knowledge, that knowledge will generally be replicated amongst all of your peers.

What distinguishes you from peer group is the character you demonstrate while you acquit your duties. It is those character qualities which will provide the underlying framework for your reputation, your career advancement, your ability to gain and keep clients and your success as a lawyer.

This list could be pretty long, but I have highlighted what I consider to be the "big ticket" items.

# Integrity

Integrity is first on my list of qualities for a reason: it's one of the most important.

All things considered, your ability maintain your integrity irrespective of the circumstances in which you find yourself will provide not only a strong backbone for your decision making, but will also earn you the respect of your colleagues and clients.

Integrity is, in essence, the character of being honest and morally upright.

From a lawyer's perspective, you have a legal duty of frankness and candour with your client, other parties and with the Court.

As a lawyer, your ability to practice is also dependant upon you being a "fit and proper person" to hold a practicing certificate from your State Law Society. If for any reason it is determined that you are not a fit and proper person, your career prospects become very grim.

As an aside, you will also only be admitted to the legal profession if you are a fit and proper person to practise. Behaviour or characteristics which adversely impact that will likely all come back to haunt you in your admission, where you are required to declare under oath that there are no issues affecting your ability to practice. Criminal records, university misbehaviour and many other issues can come up during these hearings.

Integrity, however, runs deeper than your strict legal obligations.

Integrity can be difficult to define in abstract terms, and so I will provide some practical examples:

A lawyer in charge of a file inadvertently breaches an undertaking, which was signed off by the partner. The lawyer then leaves the firm, and the breach is found out later by the partner on reviewing the file. Although the breach would never come to anybody's attention, the partner informs the Court of the breach and the circumstances. The partner is sanctioned as a result, given that the partner was notionally responsible for the entire group's work.

You become aware that a client has lied to you and to the Court in an affidavit (this is a document in Court proceedings that is sworn under oath by the client as being true). The client refuses to give you instructions to correct the position before the Court, and tells you that they will move their lucrative matter and all of their legal business to another firm unless you press on with the falsehood. You refuse to do so.

You form a view that an ethical obligation prevents you from doing a particular task that you have been assigned. After confirming that view, you take the step of informing your supervisor of the ethical issue and your concern. The partner re-assigns the work to another person and gives you no positive reassurance of any kind. Your job may be at risk as a result.

As can be seen, choosing integrity is not always the easy path – in fact, it is often the opposite.

It is simple for us to say "yes I'm an honest person and I have great integrity" until we are challenged with the cost of integrity in the face of adversity. Watch when the real pressure mounts as those with true integrity are sorted from those who do not. Watch as excuses replace honesty and rationalisation begins to creep in so that professional "face" can be saved rather than frankness and candour prevailing. Finger pointing, blame shifting and scape-goating (I'm not entirely sure that is a verb, but I'm using it anyway) when things go wrong are all indicators of a lack of integrity.

Those who maintain their integrity will always find more career satisfaction than those who do not, even after the costs of that are factored in.

If you do not start with an emphasis on the fundamental character of integrity, no amount of reading the Solicitors' Conduct Rules will create in you some kind of artificial morality to replace that which you lack.

# Flexibility

Each day, I generally start off with an idea of what I intend to do that day, and the order in which I intend to do it.

If I am lucky, that plan lasts until about midday, by which time external events have overtaken my careful planning and my list of priorities has significantly shifted.

That is the nature of legal practice, which requires you to remain calm and flexible, allowing yourself and your priorities to shift as required. It also means that you must be sensitive to the requirements of those around you in order to ensure that you are mindful of the competing priorities of others within the firm.

For example, if one secretary does your work and that of your colleague, you can expect on any given day that one or the other of you will have work that is "urgent". Both of you independently informing your secretary that the work is extremely urgent and must take priority above the others will result only in your secretary going nuts.

Instead, you must accept that a discussion about priorities is necessary, and that the highest urgency and most important work should be done first. Sometimes that will be your work, and sometimes it will not. It may mean that someone is pulled in to do overflow work for your secretary or that other resources require reallocation. In those circumstances, everyone maintaining a level of flexibility is needed.

# Focus

Focus in this context is the ability to concentrate on a task until it is complete. It is an incredibly difficult trait to maintain, but one which is of high importance in a legal career for a number of reasons.

As a law clerk, trainee/graduate or solicitor you will experience almost every day the tug of competing interests. If you give way to each, then you will find yourself drifting like a leaf in gale winds –

full of activity but otherwise not achieving anything in particular or aiming for (or reaching) a deliberate destination.

By far and away the most efficient way to complete a task is to pick it up, focus on it, work at it, and complete it – with no intermissions or diversions along the way.

This ideal method of efficiency is heavily tempered by reality (and the concept of flexibility discussed above). The fact is that you will have multiple priorities at any given time in legal practice. Focus allows you to complete the highest priority task without allowing your mind, your interests or your energy to be diverted to the other tasks until the appropriate time.

Once the highest priority task is complete, then you focus on the next (and so on).

Regrettably one of the downsides of social media has been a growth of the belief that multiple tasks can be performed simultaneously without a loss of quality. That belief is false.

Although you can review 600 "tweets", carry on 16 conversations (and I use the term loosely) on SnapChat and update your Facebook wall at basically the same time, you cannot do so with all receiving your full attention at the same time. The quality of your spelling, your comprehension, your wisdom (that is – deciding whether your communication should be made at all) and your recollection are all impacted upon by the splitting of your attention to multiple tasks.

Compare this with a face to face conversation with 1 person. You can focus on that person, deliberately and appropriately communicate with them, and ultimately make better decisions and have better recall of what was discussed.

The reality is that even the brightest and best lawyers have only a limited amount of mental power, despite what they might tell each other. Although it is inevitable that you will have multiple issues running through your mind at any given time, the ability to focus as much of your capacity as possible onto a single task at a time will serve you well.

# Self-Discipline

*"You see, some lawyers have the talent,*
*have the charisma, but no discipline. They come*
*into court unprepared, without having done*
*their research" -Nancy Grace*

Along with focus comes discipline. Discipline, in this context, is the quality of being able to systematically use your willpower to accomplish something, irrespective of the short term cost.

Physical exercise (a specific discipline with which I am personally unfamiliar, but one which many young lawyers these days seem to enjoy) is a good example. There is discipline involved in getting up each morning to attend the gym. Initially there may be pain involved, however it is discipline to continue going to the gym, ultimately to achieve the longer term benefit of improved health.

A similar path exists with study. We "hit the books" in preference to going to a mate's party, not because it is more fun to read the "equity as a sword" principle for the 28th time, but because we expect that doing so (and thereby missing out on the fun at the party) is likely to cause better academic results, which in turn will get us a better job (I should say that I make no assertion as to whether better university results in fact improve your job quality – that is a discussion point of itself).

Self-discipline in the practice of law is an important quality for a number of reasons.

Firstly, as we have seen from my list earlier, not every task that lawyers do is fun. In particular, the list of tasks completed by clerks and trainees often tends towards the less exciting aspects of the practice of law. That said, those tasks are no less important simply because they are less exciting, and they need to be performed with diligence.

A lack of self-discipline in performing those "uninteresting" jobs will have massive consequences, not just for the matter in question but for your own legal career. After all, if you cannot excel at those tasks, why would anybody give you a more challenging (and potentially more interesting) task?

## Discretion

Lawyers LOVE to tell war stories about their more illustrious legal victories: normally to each other, and often with little resemblance to the actual facts.

Most non-lawyers have a tendency to nod off to sleep somewhere a few minutes into the war story, but other lawyers find them quite entertaining. Normally war stories are also a chance for a bit of good humoured one-upmanship.

That said – good lawyers know the boundaries of what should be told as a war story, and what stays in the "vault".

On the technical side – you have legal obligations of privilege and confidentiality that you must uphold. Breaching these legal obligations will have serious negative consequences for you.

On the practical side – if you have no discretion, you will not be trusted with information. That will go for clients as well as practitioners.

If you think that telling a client a good old "confidential" war story about another client is a good way to get business or make friends – be careful. Somewhere in the back of that client's mind they are thinking "if they're prepared to tell me all this, then what do they tell other people about MY business". That is not to say there is no place for selling your expertise through previous experiences, but the details must be carefully confined.

Ultimately as a lawyer you must be a trusted advisor. If people cannot trust you, then you've lost 50% of that job description.

# THE LEGAL CAREER PATH

This section is designed to give you a brief overview of the various roles which exist within private practice (that is, at a law firm). Often different labels are used, but the career path of a lawyer in private practice follows this general series of positions.

Assuming you don't change careers mid-stream, the big picture looks something like this:

- Complete High School;

- Get a Law Degree;

- Complete Practical Legal training and whatever other requirements exist in your jurisdiction to become a lawyer;

- Be "admitted" as a lawyer (having completed the necessary requirements, this involves an application to the Court by somebody on your behalf, and a nice little ceremonial hearing whereby the Court grants an application for your admission to the legal profession)

- Either upon the above step, or some time before it, get a job;

- Get promoted to a point where you don't want to (or can't) be promoted anymore;

- Retire and spend your time annoying your grandchildren by pretending that you are deaf.

Primarily this section is about the second last step, although some of the earlier job titles could be throughout your university study.

As this is the "professional practice" list I have not included administrative roles like legal assistant or office assistant, although many lawyers have worked in these roles at some point.

Similarly I have not included government positions or in-house positions, as these follow a different path and, while perfectly legitimate paths to take, are not the norm for the majority of law graduates.

# Law Clerk

This is where you work for a firm providing general administrative and legal research tasks. You will often be required to do Court filing, to answer research requests, to compile or index documents. You may also be called on for the "needle in a haystack" style tasks of document review, where a fact or issue is sought to be identified via the review of a lot of material.

During this phase, you will probably have a low-ish charge out rate (that is, the price that the firm charges you out to clients at) and a similarly low salary.

In terms of work you will likely answer to solicitors, associates, senior associates, special counsel and partners (yes – that's nearly everyone). Officially, you will probably have a partner or senior associate as your supervisor.

Your job will likely involve working with legal assistants at various times, but not necessarily having one as "your assistant". Bear in mind that during this time the chances that an experienced legal secretary knows more about the practice of law than you do are pretty high.

Where you can excel here is by:

- Diligently doing what you have been asked to do;
- Paying attention to how senior lawyers conduct files, and learning accordingly;
- Showing an appropriate level of initiative;
- Having a positive attitude towards work and your colleagues;
- Meeting deadlines;
- Being honest with your capacity – don't say you can do something if you can't;
- Paying attention and taking notes when somebody is giving you instructions. It is not "against the rules" to ask for clarification of instructions, but if you've simply forgotten what you were asked to do, then that's not good;
- Understanding the hierarchy of the firm and where you are in it (towards the bottom, if you were wondering).

First impressions last, remember. The position of law clerk is essentially a filter for the firm to figure out who they are going to hire later as a lawyer. That said, it is not always a "thumbs down" if you are not hired later – it may simply be that there were no positions on offer when the time came.

# Trainee Solicitor/Law Graduate

A trainee solicitor (or sometimes "law graduate") generally has completed their law degree and is in the process of practical legal training.

There will be a gradual progression in this phase from the tasks done by law clerks through to the tasks done by solicitors.

You will likely start to have your own smaller files under the supervision of a partner or senior associate.

It is in this role you need to start figuring out how to get things done with people. That means working with a secretary and working with your supervisors.

As you are still training, you will still likely be delegated more complex research tasks or other jobs which the law clerks cannot do. If there are no law clerks at your firm, then this likelihood becomes a certainty.

That said; if you are excelling in your position then over time you will likely start to receive similar treatment to that of a junior solicitor.

# Solicitor

Hooray! If you have been admitted to practice following 4-5 years of study and another year or two of training then congratulations: you are now the most junior legal practitioner in your firm!

As a solicitor you will be responsible for some of your own files. You will likely work with a Partner or Senior Associate directly who will supervise you where necessary.

In addition, you will likely now start to take on some of the administrative burden of file management, including billing, chasing payments, costs agreements and estimates, and those parts of the file which to date you have probably not been involved in.

Ultimately your job as a solicitor from an economic view is going to be to make or exceed your budget. Although you will have limited control over this, if you are light on work make sure you are communicating that to the necessary people. It is not likely that there will be expectations on you to bring work in from a marketing standpoint.

As a solicitor you will probably start producing from scratch more work that is going to be seen externally (letters of advice, pleadings in Court matters etc). Do not take amendments on your drafts as criticisms, even if red ink has basically been poured onto every line. It is this period where you need to start paying attention to the particular writing styles of the various people for whom you work, and tailoring your work accordingly. There are many ways to skin a cat – until you can have your own way, your job is to produce something that the Partners will sign. Amendments are the way you learn those preferences.

As a solicitor you can excel by:

- Dealing appropriately with administrative staff, junior and senior professional staff;

- Showing an appropriate level of initiative (yes – this was on the last list as well, but what is "appropriate" may have now changed);

- Having a good understanding of the administrative tasks required to run files;

- Knowing, and abiding by, your ethical duties (which by now are hopefully second nature);

- Understanding your role in the firm and in your group. This will vary from case to case, so it may require you to have a conversation with somebody to figure out what is expected of you in a more practical way than just "be a solicitor";

- Understanding how estimates work. If your firm estimates that providing an advice will cost $2,000, and you chew up $1900 (or more) of that to get a draft done, then it's a problem. You need to allow for your work to be reviewed and finalised. How much that will cost depends on the nature of the task. If you think the estimate is too low, then speak with your supervisor;

- Keeping up to date with the law. If you think that University taught you all the law you need to know, then you are wrong. In the last decade I can count on my fingers the work days where I haven't learned something new;

- Focusing on quality. Typos, incorrect law, failing to adopt the style guide and all sorts of easily avoided errors are not acceptable. Such minor errors cost the firm money, and they make you look bad. Produce your work carefully, proof read it, and only hand a document to your supervisors that you would be happy to sign and send with your own name on it;

- Focusing on efficiency. This will be a balancing act with quality. Most people could produce a perfect one page letter if they took 3 days to write, re-write and edit it. However your job is also to produce it efficiently. This means finding a pace and developing a process for work production that, for you, will produce the required outcome with minimum errors and maximum efficiency;

- Deliver on what you promise. If you tell your supervisor (or a client) that you can do something by a particular time, or date – then do it.

# Associate/Senior Associate

At this point the lines of promotion start to get a little blurry. Principally this is because of the wide disparity between different firms about when you might be eligible for these next steps.

As a (very) rough guide, most firms will require you to have completed a minimum of two, but more likely three, years post-admission experience to be made an Associate. Senior Associate will probably require another two to three years experience after that, if not more.

Some firms do not have a "Senior Associate" position. The transition will then be from Associate straight to Partner (or Special Counsel if that option exists).

The technical skills you have learned during your time as a solicitor will solidify here. That is not to say that you stop learning new things (that actually never happens) but you will now be comfortable with the fundamentals of the area you work in, able to perform many tasks without too much "hand-holding" and able to carry on discussions with clients without a greater degree of confidence.

The principle distinctions between solicitors and Associates are:

- Seniority;
- Business Development;

- Leadership.

As an Associate it is likely that you will be expected to take on some kind of deliberate and meaningful business development.

That does NOT mean, however, that you will be expected to instantly start bringing in $500k plus of work each year just to keep yourself employed. The reality is that business development takes a number of forms. What form each person engages in depends on their strengths and weaknesses, as well as the requirements of the firm.

You may, for example, be asked to do any of the following:

- Give presentations either internally or externally;
- Write articles (if you haven't been already);
- Attend "select-invite" functions (that is, not just the ones that the entire group goes to);
- Have greater contact with existing clients to ensure that they are being well looked after (yes – this IS business development and a critical component of it).

It is unlikely you'll be asked to go and have a "tête-à-tête" with the CEO of a Top 20 ASX listed company, so try to keep things in proportion.

However, this period is a fantastic opportunity to start, or continue, developing relationships with others in areas that you might like one day to practice in. You might not get a meeting with the top boss, but if you have solid relationships with your non-legal peers, then you can reasonably expect that around the time you start making more significant business decisions, they will be doing the same.

In terms of leadership, as an Associate you will be expected to show a certain amount of solidarity and commitment when it comes to team-building and group maintenance. You might be responsible for managing a legal secretary, or possibly a trainee or junior solicitor. This is a chance for you to demonstrate how you go at building a team which, ultimately, will be what you need to have if you are going to be a Partner.

As an Associate/Senior Associate you can excel by:

- Understanding the business development expectations that the firm has for you;

- Demonstrating your ability to ensure that clients are happy with your work;

- Participating in administrative functions (eg committees etc) and marketing endeavours within your area of expertise;

- Mentoring junior staff either formally or informally;

- Starting to learn about firm economics, billing, running a business, marketing and other non-legal areas where you may not have had any exposure to this point. These are all required knowledge if you are going to ultimately own a business (ie –

Partnership) – you might as well start to understand how a firm actually functions;

- Exercising appropriate supervision of your legal assistant and junior staff;

- Demonstrating an understanding of appropriate delegation (or "leverage").

- As to the distinction between Senior Associate and Associate? That's a bit tough, but here are some possibilities:

- Senior Associates will generally have more administrative, leadership and business development burden than Associates;

- Senior Associates may be responsible for bringing in a certain amount of work, or have a greater expectation on them to be trying to generate relationships for that purpose;

- Senior Associates are likely to have Partnership somewhere "in their sights";

- Senior Associates will likely have conduct of their own files and limited authority to sign letters, although still subject to Partner supervision where required.

# Special Counsel

I have to tread cautiously here, because Special Counsel is a role of an ambiguous nature.

Special Counsel was a role traditionally given to senior practitioners (Senior Associate level or higher) who did not wish to be Partners, and/or had no interest in developing a practice of their own.

It can also be a role where firms who had a bottleneck in promotions (ie – lots of Senior Associates but no intention of adding any Partners) would make a promotion to Special Counsel in order to stave off mass resignations from disgruntled Senior Associates who were being held out of Partnership.

The final possibility was that it was a role offered to somebody who the firm valued as an employee of technical skill, but for one reason or another the firm had determined that they were not likely to make that person a partner.

These days, however, I strongly caution against making any kind of assumption about what "Special Counsel" can mean, as it can be different both between firms and within them.

Absent the characteristic of seniority (it is, in all cases, a role for senior practitioners) the specifics of why any particular person might have the position are up to you to figure out tactfully.

# Salaried Partner/Equity Partner

So this is what lots of aspiring lawyers are actually aspiring to: Partnership.

These days it might have one of a few possible labels: Director, Principal, Partner. Those are just different names for different firm structures.

When will you make Partner? I have no idea. The days of completing your clerkship and then being offered partnership when you recover from your post-admission hangover are gone.

Every firm will have its own expectations, whether they be written or unwritten, and you will have to find out what they are at some point. All I can set out for you here are some general expectations that most firms will have for those who wish to be Partners:

- All the positive qualities that I have tried to set out in the previous areas;
- A demonstrated ability to gain and keep clients, and a stated desire to continue on that path;
- Profitable fee generation of a significant amount. Likely this will have to be enough to keep you and at least one other junior lawyer person busy, although there is no set rule;
- Technical excellence;

- The ability to effectively lead a team of professional and support staff;

- Appropriate delegation of tasks;

- No, or minimal, significant client complaints of any merit;

- Supervision and management skills;

- An understanding of how the firm works, both politically and practically;

- Completion of the Practice Management Course (note – this is a Queensland Law Society requirement for principals of firms);

- An acceptance and adoption of the firm's culture and general values;

- The ability to work in concert with the existing partners.

I won't set out "how to excel" as a partner, because I've never tried it and that's probably another book (one that's likely already been written – a few times) in itself.

Rest assured that Partnership is, however, hard work. It is also pre-loaded with stress.

After all, as a Partner, the buck stops with you. If you sign it – it's your fault. If you don't supervise properly – it's your fault. If you don't bring in the work, then you get to pick who has to be fired as a consequence. If you bring in more work, then you do the hiring. You are responsible for keeping your team productive and at their best, for maintaining client relationships, for answering client complaints, for reviewing bills, for managing finances and debtors, for spending the marketing budget (if there is one) or explaining why you overspent the marketing budget.

Some Partners are natural rainmakers (this term is used for people who have the ability to bring in significant volumes of work in professional services). Others are not. Some Partners are excellent group leaders and people managers, and others are not. Some are administratively anal retentive (this sounds like a criticism but my view is that it is a good thing) and others look like a bomb hits their office every morning. Some partners micro manage and others are so casual that you wonder if they actually read your draft letters at all.

The point of this is that there is no specific quality or characteristic of a "Partner" that I can hold up as a target for you. As a Partner you do what needs doing. If you do it well, then hopefully you can keep doing it well. If you don't, or if you lose heart, then perhaps you should have applied for that Special Counsel position they offered you...

A "salaried Partner" is one whose income is not dependant on the profits of the business. They are a partner in name, but do not share in the ownership. They are sometimes called a "fixed draw" partner.

An "equity Partner" is one who actually owns a piece of the business. Therefore, their income depends upon the profitability and revenue of the firm as a whole.

It has become more normal for a practitioner to first transition to a salaried Partner position, and then later to an equity Partner position once they have solidified their practice and their team, and can demonstrate an overall contribution to the firm such that the other equity Partners want them "on board".

In order to make the transition to an equity Partner, it is likely that you will need to buy into the firm. Yes – you will need to pay money. After all, you are purchasing a piece of the business, and in one sense it is no different to buying shares in a company – why should it be a gift? Often Partnerships will allow the purchase price to be paid back as a withholding from the dividends that you earn in the business, but ultimately the deal itself will be on a case by case and firm by firm basis. You'll need to work that out as you get closer.

# Barrister/Judge

I haven't listed these at this point because I consider them the next stages of "promotion", but largely to acknowledge that the roles of Barrister and Judge are perfectly legitimate and alternative goals to those which I have set out above. They are, however, positions in relation to which I have no personal exposure and so it wouldn't be appropriate for me to go commenting on them. If you are interested in becoming a Barrister (whether or not with a view to later becoming a Judge) then I suggest you try and find a friendly Barrister and buy them a coffee in exchange for a bit of wisdom.

# NEGATIVES OF LEGAL WORK

Yep – being a lawyer has a down side.

Shocking, isn't it?

I've set out a couple of big ticket items here to ensure that I've mentioned them. I have no doubt there are more.

## Stress

Stress is pretty common for the legal professional. I'm not sure of the exact catalyst for it, but generally it seems to stem from high work loads combined with demanding clients/supervisors.

Neither of those things can be avoided all the time. You can manage your workload to an extent, just as your supervisors will (if they are realistic) try to manage how demanding they are of your time.

Your clients will sometimes have little appreciation for the amount of work that has to go into the product that they have requested, and so you might be on the receiving end of unreasonable timeframes more than a few times.

That said, stress is not about the situation you are in so much as it is about how you react to that situation.

If you deal with stress poorly (by which I mean you become incapable of coherent thought) then you might need to train yourself to deal with it better. I'm sure there are books or courses on the topic, but this isn't one of them.

If you are a student then let me make this clear: the stress of study week, exam periods, assignment due dates – are absolutely nothing next to the potential for stress in a legal career. Your high school and university educations have been carefully managed to be as reasonable as humanly possible.

Your legal career will offer you no such indulgences. I say this not to frighten you, but simply so that you understand the relatively calm waters of your legal studies bear no real resemblance to the squall that is the legal profession.

The issue is one of control. In your studies you knew what was coming, when it was coming, generally what it would involve, and you had plenty of time to prepare for it. As a lawyer, you can try to plan all you want, but as often as not the unexpected will happen, the emergency will occur, and all of a sudden you will be up a particular creek without a particular instrument.

Not being a counsellor in any way (that's a disclaimer, in case you missed it), my personal suggestions for avoiding or at least limiting stress build up are:

- If you have done something wrong or made a mistake – own up to it immediately and deal with it;
- If you feel your workload becoming overwhelming, inform somebody sooner rather than later;

- Learn to say that you are too busy to do something before accepting it;

- Don't accept multiple urgent tasks at the same time without clarifying with the relevant people which is more urgent;

- Accept that clients calling something urgent doesn't always mean that it is. Sometimes it does, and sometimes it can wait a day in favour of the more urgent task;

- Have an outlet that is unrelated to legal practice – take up a hobby, do sport or whatever (note – drinking heavily is NOT an outlet);

- Stay focused and disciplined. Don't let stress diminish your preferred approach to legal practice;

- If personal issues are affecting your work life, take some leave and sort them out.

# Hours

Lawyers work hard.

I think that probably every law clerk/trainee solicitor has, at one point, calculated their hourly pay and compared it to what the person who cooks the fries at McDonalds or pushes the trolleys at Coles earns.

It is a sobering comparison.

The reality is that the hours you work are an investment into your legal career, and not instantaneously financially rewarding.

Most lawyers I know work between 40 and 50 hours (excluding lunch breaks) per week. Many work up to 55 hours per week, and a few work 60 hours or more per week. I am not aware of any firm that would expect a professional staff member to work less than 40 hours a week unless they are part time.

Terms like "overtime" don't really exist in the legal profession. Occasionally after a period of long work hours the more benevolent partners might allow a practitioner a day or two off as a thank you.

Many lawyers choose to consistently work extremely long hours of their own volition. That's fine, provided you don't pretend that makes you superior to those who don't make that same choice. It just makes you some person who has nothing better to do at the end of the day than to keep working.

If, however, you find your hours are both overwhelming and involuntary, then there are only a few likely possibilities for why:

- It's trial preparation (or some similar short term insanity) and all hands are on deck for that period in the knowledge that it will end some time soon so you can get some well earned time off;

- You have bitten off more than you can chew and your general workload is too high;

- You are working inefficiently.

Hopefully you can identify the first fairly easily, but distinguishing between the second and third points can sometimes be a challenge.

If you find that a lot of your time is being written off (that is – fees you put on your time sheet but don't get billed to the client) then you might be working inefficiently. By "a lot" I mean probably anything more than 10% of your time. The write off percentage should go down as you become more senior. Ideally it should be a lot lower, but if it is consistently higher than that you need to find out why. Speak with your supervising Partner and discuss why the time is being written off, to see if they can offer any guidance.

If you have said "yes" to too much work, then you need to own up unless you are going to swiftly remedy it. Working extremely long hours and missing out on a necessary recharge is a risk-filled recipe for disaster, not just for you but for the firm. If it lasts more than a short time you need to get some of those files out of your control and re-delegated. You also need to learn from that experience to predict better what your workload is going to be so it doesn't happen again.

Most lawyers have found themselves overburdened at one time or another. However, if consistently long hours or long work are wearing you down and impacting on your performance, then you need to do something about it.

I should say that some lawyers seem to thrive on working all the time. Again, if that is by choice and isn't causing them to gradually have a mental breakdown, then no worries from me.

You'll notice that I place a lot of emphasis in this section on you. I do accept that there are some firms (and some individual Partners) who expect their young lawyers to work simply unbelievable hours. Such firms ordinarily come with associated rewards, whether they be money, prestige or tangible perks. If not, they probably come with a high staff turnover.

If the culture of your firm is to work insanely long hours and you don't like it – the options are obvious: change your opinion about the hours; work there and limit your hours (this could have consequences); or leave. I'm not a big fan of the "sitting around and whining about it" approach to such things, but if that's how you choose to deal with a situation, then don't expect it to actually change.

# Conflict

Conflict is an inevitable part of legal practice for a number of reasons. Before I get into those reasons though, let's be clear what we are talking about.

Not all conflict is bad. In fact much conflict is necessary, healthy and productive (I know that I could have just said "good" there, but I chose to use 3 words instead of 1 – after all, I am a lawyer). Take two lawyers who disagree about the appropriate strategy for a client. They discuss the issues, weigh the pros and cons, and ultimately a decision is made having considered the relevant options. That is healthy conflict, which is not the topic of this section.

This section is more about "bad" conflict – the kind that has no rational beginning and doesn't really have a rational way of ending.

If you are going to work with other people, the chances are fairly high that there will be conflict. The chances are raised further in law firms in particular is because there are times of high workload, high stress, and low margin for error.

Here are some obvious examples of "bad" conflict:

- Person A decides that Person B doesn't work hard enough. Person A then spends half their daily energy on telling everybody about it, while Person B then feels victimized. Persons C through F in the team find the entire issue distracting and annoying;

- Person A begrudges Person B a promotion or some other opportunity because they "didn't deserve it". Person A has a whinge as often as possible. Person B "takes it out" on Person A by giving them all of the worst jobs they can think of. Person A and Person B end up in a constant series of arguments about childish issues that distract the entire team.

To me there is really only one solution to "bad" conflict – somebody has to get over it.

I nominate YOU. Given a choice, YOU should always be the "bigger person". Other people's problems are their own. Re-read my section on "Power and Influence" earlier if you don't think it will make any difference.

If conflict, however, is turning in to bullying or harassment, then you may need to do something more considered about it. I'm not going to go in to detail on this, but if you believe that things have crossed that line, then you will need to speak to somebody about it, hopefully sooner rather than later. Sometimes that is the HR department, sometimes it is a trusted senior person in the firm. Sometimes, unfortunately, little gets done about such things on an institutional level, and you may need to consider changing teams or jobs.

# POSITIVES OF LEGAL WORK

Above I have listed some negatives of legal work. Thankfully they are ordinarily surmountable or manageable, which means that you have an opportunity to focus on the positives.

Again – below are just a few out of many.

## Stimulation

A legal career is highly stimulating. Hopefully if you're still reading you have already decided on your motivating factors to become a lawyer. Well – if you've done that right, then your chosen career can provide all the stimulation you need.

Here are a few areas where I personally find a legal career to be awesome:

- Urgency – nothing gets the blood going like having an urgent deadline, a swift Court hearing, an advice on a complex area required in short order, or some other form of "quick DO IT NOW". Although this can be debilitating for some, provided the deadlines are achievable I find this process to be quite rewarding. You get to sit back at the end and say "look how well we pulled that together".

- Intellectual stimulation – I've dealt with this in detail earlier in this book. However, despite the dull times, I personally find the process of trying to hunt out a technical answer to a tricky question to be very rewarding.

- High value – many legal deals or disputes relate to high (sometimes massively high) value matters. Being involved in a dispute about $127,000,000 is a big deal. The number in itself provides a certain motivation and stimulation for your ongoing conduct.

- High profile – although not too common, there may well be matters where the media or other interests are involved. Generally you won't get to comment, but the fact that other people are actually interested in your work for a change offers its own level of encouragement.

- Breaking New Ground – I have been fortunate enough to be involved in a few matters which have sought to clarify or define a law that was previously unclear. Connected with intellectual stimulation, the concept of actually using your skills of statutory interpretation rather than just "looking for a precedent" provides for some interesting discussions, interesting cases, and very interesting decisions.

# Relationship

Legal careers are highly social. You will not in any way feel like you are lacking human interaction in your time as a lawyer.

If you are lucky (from this phrase, you will correctly infer that I am a bit of an introvert) you will get a brief stint of peace at the start (and possibly the end) of the day. In between, however, you will have plenty of discussions and communications to keep you busy.

All aspects of legal work are founded in the need for relationship.

If you need a cheque drawn – you probably need to ask your assistant to do up a cheque request, who will then have the partner sign off on it, and then take it to accounts department, who will ultimately draw the cheque which will be delivered back to your assistant by either accounts or another support staff member of some kind. The simple task of drawing a cheque offers the opportunity to interact with 4 other people in the process. It is like this with all tasks.

Similarly you will have meetings and conferences involving multiple personalities and plenty of chance for interaction.

Clients, ultimately, will come to you if you develop relationship with them. Although part of that involves delivering legal services well, they will not ultimately choose to engage you (most of the time) unless they also feel some degree of personal connection with you.

Similarly, you will build a team of people around you by developing relationships.

Having a circle of people with whom you have close relationships is a powerful positive influence. It offers you the chance to have diverse and varied conversations at different levels of complexity and from a range of different perspectives.

Even for an introvert, the building of relationships is, in my view, a positive outcome of a legal career.

## Service

At the risk of becoming overly philosophical in what is supposed to be a factual (or at least opinionated) book, I think the service element is a positive part of a legal career.

I have not yet met anybody who does not desire to make some kind of impact on the world around them. A legal career gives you the chance to do that.

In serving your firm and your clients well, you get that nice "warm fuzzy feeling" associated with a job well done. If you are performing your tasks diligently and with integrity, carrying out your client's instructions astutely, and (hopefully) securing a "win" every now and again, then you do start to develop a genuinely positive feeling towards going to work each day.

The feeling of coming off a win from a big matter (be it a trial or a transaction) with a satisfied client is a very rewarding experience. It is at this point that all the hard work you have put in pays off and yields the rewards.

Occasionally, of course, things do go a bit pear shaped and your client isn't always happy. Provided you have done your job and performed your tasks as best you can – there's nothing you can do about that.

As I have said earlier, legal training also offers you the chance to serve in other areas of the community. I know many lawyers who choose to serve the community in a variety of different ways, and all of them find that it gives them a profound sense of satisfaction.

# TYPES OF LAW FIRM

If you've gotten to this point and haven't been put off by some of the stark realities of legal practice, then this section is a very quick summary of the different sizes of law firm, and some of the potential benefits and pitfalls of each. These are general comments only – there are really no set rules here, and the sheer variety of firms makes it nearly impossible to write anything that holds true in all circumstances.

For most firms where I have worked, of the total numbers of staff normally around 50% are legally trained, and the balance are administrative and support staff (including marketing people, accounts people and legal secretaries). The numbers I use below are total staff, not just the lawyers.

I don't subscribe to the view that "bigger is better". Bigger firms come with some benefits, but they also have some associated burdens. Which size/category of firm is the best match for your personality will be an entirely personal decision.

## Boutique/Small Firm

The word "boutique" when it comes to law firms is often just a nicer way of saying "small" without using a word that has connotations of negativity. Sometimes you might find that a firm describing itself as "boutique" is seeking to establish itself (or has established itself) as a specialist in a particular niche area.

Generally I would categorise a firm as "small" if it had less than around 40 people all together. There is no particular rule about what a small firm is or is not, so that number is arbitrary.

One of the greatest benefits (in career terms, at least) of working in a smaller firm is that you are frequently given a higher level of responsibility and exposure to clients. The experience you gain will be at the "coal face" more than those of your peers who go to larger firms.

You will also face less bureaucracy in terms of decision making than you do at a larger firm (ie – if you want a new pen, then just get one, rather than having to fill out a form to requisition a stationary re-supply order which will arrive in 2 weeks time).

On the flip side, smaller firms have a tendency to command less sophisticated clients, and less complex matters. So although your legal experience will be significant, you are less likely to be exposed to large, complex disputes with clients of significant size. That is not always a bad thing, but it can mean that there are greater problems with cash flow, clients paying bills and other administrative matters in smaller law firms.

You may or may not have a legal secretary in a smaller firm – often solicitors in smaller firms are fairly autonomous in terms of their work output. As people become more proficient with technology, this issue is not necessarily inefficient for the client, but that's really a case by case assessment.

Because of the lower income stream, smaller firms also frequently face tighter budgets when it comes to things like client entertainment and library costs. Although this concept may be alien to those of you who are law students, the nearly unlimited resources which you so freely enjoy as part of your studies cost an absolutely atrocious amount of money when it comes to the commercial sector. Commercial reality can mean that previously simple tasks like getting copies of cases, researching legal principles and the like can be more difficult.

Finally, the reality of smaller firms is that you may well be paid less than in the larger firm counterparts.

In all, my personal experience is that people who have trained in smaller firms, working under partners who have taken an interest in their staff's development, have a wonderful starting platform for their careers.

## Mid-Tier Firms

A "mid-tier" firm (or medium sized firm) is one with generally between 40 and 150 people all together.

Often a mid-tier firm will have more than one office, but not necessarily have a full national presence.

At this point you are likely to be competitive (although not quite equal) in terms of pay structure for the larger firms. You are also likely to have good resources available to you, although not necessarily comprehensive in terms of research, library and the like.

The chances are that if you are born after 1990 you will be unhappy with the computer system, unless you are lucky enough to be working somewhere that has just upgraded. The fact is that upgrading computer systems for 150 people is really expensive, and often unnecessary for the type of work done in offices anyway.

In terms of support, mid-tier firms are more likely than smaller firms to have dedicated marketing staff, and also a more sophisticated accounts section to deal with the money issues.

The downside is that as there are more people, a more regimented system of operation generally comes in to play. Rather than whole firm mentality, the chances are that you will have workgroups (or divisions, or whatever) into which the firm is split, each with a partner or partners to lead the relevant team of people in a particular legal area. Those groups will each have their own budgets, and often their own culture in terms of how people interact with each other.

Related to the above, as a junior staff member you will still get some exposure to clients and real legal issues, but not the same kind of "thrown in the deep end" approach that you may have enjoyed at a smaller firm. There will be a more rigid structure around who can do what, and to manage risk in these larger firms they need to ensure that most work is supervised or reviewed by more senior staff.

Mid-tier firms are also likely to come with larger clients, and in the current market are often competitive with the very large firms in terms of government work and large public company work. They do this by having the structure, expertise and size to take on large matters with a variety of legal issues but not necessarily the associated hourly charge out rates that larger firms have.

# Top-Tier/Large Firms

These are firms with (generally) more than 150 people.

To gain the label "top-tier" it is generally accepted that the firm must have a total national presence – that is, it must be able to serve clients in every state and territory. In Australia, most main offices for top-tier firms are in Sydney or Melbourne, and the other offices around the country generally have less people than those main areas.

That said, there are in most States still large firms which are not necessarily "top-tier". These are firms which have reached a significant size without deciding to expand themselves (and taking on the associated administrative burden) to all of the other States.

Working in a large firm you will likely find that all the differences between small and medium sized firms start to become more accentuated. Specifically, role designation and authorization will be more important (ie – who can do what, or sign what). Similarly, you will likely have a larger marketing and accounting team in the larger firm.

Large or top-tier firms often come with top-tier clients and top-tier matters. This may sound like a wonderful thing, but can have its associated problems.

There is a classic example for junior lawyers in litigation circles, which is that of disclosure. Disclosure is the process of analysing, compiling and listing all documents that your client has which are relevant to a dispute (and also the process of looking at the other side's version of the same thing). In a small matter, disclosure is a burden. In a very large matter, disclosure can be a nightmare. Disclosure is also generally the task which is done by junior lawyers. So while the idea of being involved in a $100m claim sounds pretty exciting, it can become less so when you realize that there are 50 archive boxes of documents which you need to go through, page by page, to assess relevance and put in chronological order.

At the large size, basic events like firm-wide celebrations or whatever can become extremely difficult to organise, and so you will often find that social events are often held on a workgroup basis. There will still be firm wide functions, but they will be less frequent by virtue of their logistical challenges.

At a large firm you would expect to be on the higher end of the salary bracket. You will also find that this comes with expectations in terms of work hours and dedication.

One of the most common complaints about the very large firms has been that partnership is very hard to access. Competition for partnership can be quite fierce, and I know a number of people who have been caught in the "work harder, longer" race to get to the top, in an effort to distinguish themselves from their peers. The unfortunate reality is that there are not always as many partnership positions available as there are people who want them – as a result, some people find themselves disappointed.

# CONCLUSION

Hopefully I have offered you an honest and relatively comprehensive review of what a legal career can look like, the characteristics of good lawyers, and some traits you might reflect on.

The decision to pursue a legal career has a lot of potential variations, and here I have really only offered insight into one of them – being a career in private practice. Your legal skills will serve you well in many fields, however, from management to HR to marketing to corporate boards to charities to politics and many more.

With that in mind you might decide to leap in, guns blazing, to a life in the law – but ultimately realize that some aspects of it don't work for you the way you thought they would, and leave to pursue something different.

That's OK. It happens, and everybody I know in such a position has survived such a decision to enjoy their future career with some experience under their belts and a different perspective on life.

I trust you will go on to a career that fulfills you. If that is the law – then maybe I'll see you in Court!

# ABOUT THE AUTHOR

Towards the end of my secondary schooling I decided that a law degree was my best option. For a long time I was headed towards engineering or the sciences, but for various reasons thought that a legal career might hold greater interest for me.

As it turns out, I was right (not through my own wise decision making, but by the providence of God). Although a slightly disinterested law student, I found (and still find) that the practice of law with its real world issues is a thoroughly enjoyable and fulfilling career.

I have been working in law firms now for over 10 years. I started in a smaller practice, worked in a medium sized firm for over 5 years, and now work in a larger law firm. At each stage I have had the privilege of working with people of integrity and significant talent, who took the time and had the patience to invest into my life with their greater experience and knowledge.

I wrote this particular book because I hoped it might help those in the early stages of their career to have a good grounding to identify and articulate their own motivations and shape their careers. For my part, I am at a stage now where I am looking to use what I can to help young(er) people who are training to be lawyers or just starting their careers. I find investing into the lives of young lawyers to be a rewarding and beneficial way to spend my time, and I hope to continue doing so for a long time to come.

I can be contacted through a number of means, but the easiest are:

My Website: http://www.tipsforlawyers.com

Twitter: https://twitter.com/joyouslawyer

LinkedIn: http://au.linkedin.com/pub/chris-hargreaves/23/b22/768/

Google+: https://plus.google.com/u/0/+ChrisHargreaves1/

Facebook: https://www.facebook.com/tipsforlawyers

Email: chris@tipsforlawyers.com

www.ingramcontent.com/pod-product-compliance
Lightning Source LLC
Chambersburg PA
CBHW060324220326

41598CB00027B/4410